BE HAPPY!

How to Stop Negative Thinking, Start Focusing on
the Positive, and Create Your Happiness Mindset

NICOLE FISHER

Be Happy! - How to Stop Negative Thinking, Start Focusing on the Positive, and Create Your Happiness Mindset

Nicole Fisher

Copyright 2012 by Empowerment Nation

EmpowermentNation.com

Table of Contents

__Introduction__

Happiness. Who couldn't use a little more of it? Be truthful. When was the last time you were truly happy? I mean really, *really* happy. Some people seem to be naturally happy, regardless of their circumstances. It can be humbling, to say the least, to see those less fortunate than ourselves as they seemingly drift along, content and joyful in simple pursuits, while we struggle to maintain an even keel. What is their secret?

Contrary to what you might believe, you can be happy – or happier – than what you are at this very moment. And it's not very difficult to do. The first step in achieving happiness is redefining your thoughts on what happiness is. How do you define happiness? Do you see it as a place you can go to—a refuge of sorts? Or do you see it as a journey? If happiness is a destination, then how do you get there? If these are questions you have trouble answering, you're not alone.

This book will help you understand that happiness is really not a place at all, but rather a state of mind. Attaining happiness is a conscious decision you must make for yourself; no one can give you

1

happiness, and no one can take it away. Happiness, or the pursuit of it, is what gives us hope. Happiness and joy give our lives meaning and hold us up when things get rocky; they are the glue that holds our lives together.

This book will cover topics such as:

- The definition of happiness

- The science of happiness

- The risk of being a people pleaser

- How to develop a happy mindset

More than this, the book will also examine why some people (perhaps you're one of them) don't feel like they deserve happiness. It will also give you practical techniques to help you change your thought processes going forward, learn to find your passion and purpose, discover ways to turn a bad situation around, and methods to accept and embrace change.

Filled with wonderful analogies, this book will help you take the steps to start improving your life *right now*. So what are you waiting for? The sooner you get started, the sooner you'll discover your own path to inner peace.

Chapter One: Defining Happiness – Is That Even Possible?

The Elusive Nature of Happiness

Looking back to when you were a child, did you ever spend your time outside chasing butterflies with the hope of catching one? How many were you able to actually catch this way? If you were like most children, the answer is not very many. But after you tired yourself out and sat very still for a while, you may have been lucky enough to have had one land on you. At the very least, one fluttered gently close by. For many of us, happiness is an elusive quality. People, many experts say, are not wired for happiness; instead we are wired for survival. Many of us find ourselves rushing through life, chasing happiness; the problem with this method, though, is that we never quite get there.

Perhaps that's how you're approaching happiness – chasing it just like that elusive butterfly of your youth. You seem to be getting close to it, but it's always slightly out of reach. Does it seem as if you're destined to be unhappy for the rest of your life? Do well-intentioned, but misguided, individuals tell you with authority about the wording in the Declaration of Independence? It guarantees you "life, liberty and the pursuit of happiness." It doesn't promise you actual happiness. It just allows you to chase it all you want!

Take a moment to ask yourself if any of the following statements sound familiar:

- I'll be happy when I get out of school.

- I'll be happy when I get married.

- I'll be happy when I start making more money.

- I'll be happy when I have a child.

- I'll be happy when my children move out on their own.

- I'll finally be happy when I retire.

Before you know it, you have frittered your life away in this elusive quest, and you still haven't figured out how to be happy.

Whether or not someone is happy depends on their individual perspective. Many of us are afraid to be happy because we are so used to raw negative emotions and pain that suffering becomes a way of life. In other words, happiness is a choice. More than that, happiness is a state of mind. It is not a destination.

While many people are on a quest to be happy, the fundamental problem is that they neglect to enjoy the moment. They mistakenly believe that happiness is a goal to be achieved sometime in the future.

So exactly what does it take to have amazing happiness and peace of mind? Is it money? Possessions? A family? Success? None of these things actually guarantees happiness. Perhaps you already have a family. Before you enjoyed a family setting, you may have thought that this was the key to true happiness. Or perhaps you've spent many years cultivating a career and making a great deal of money only to discover it didn't bring you the happiness you thought. So what's missing?

Happiness Defined

The dictionary defines happiness as the quality or state of being happy; good fortune and/or joy; a state of well-being or contentment; or a pleasurable or happy experience. Some synonyms for happiness include words like: exhilaration, delight, enjoyment, satisfaction, bliss, contentment, and pleasure, to name just a few.

But that's not the end of the definition. The dictionary also tells us that happiness results from the possession or attainment of what one considers *good*.

The opposite of happiness is misery. Unfortunately, far too many individuals are familiar with this state. As well meaning as this definition is, it really isn't very helpful in helping us get to the core of the state of happiness. In your pursuit of the definition of happiness, it might help to discover how science weighs in on the subject.

The Science of Happiness

Believe it or not, the actual science of happiness is a new study in the field of psychology. Psychotherapy, first formalized by Sigmund Freud, was designed around the premise of focusing in on one's faults and agonizingly analyzing one's deep dark drives. Definitely not a recipe for happiness. The study of happiness, or as it's more formally called, positive psychology, works on a different premise altogether. Instead of dwelling on your weaknesses and fears, it emphasizes your *strengths and virtues*.

Perhaps we're on to something here. Dr. Martin Seligman, one of the founders of positive psychology, often uses happiness and well-being interchangeably. He defines happiness as both positive feelings, such as ecstasy and comfort, and positive activities that have no feeling component at all. By this, he means states of mind like absorption and engagement. A happy life, according to

Seligman, is one filled with positive feelings and activities. How often and how intensely you feel is an indication of your level of enduring or true happiness.

Could Happiness Be "Living in the Moment?"

Not "happy" with that definition? Here's another one that might be more to your liking. Dr. Barbara Fredrickson, another positive psychologist, says happiness is the fuel to thrive and flourish as well as to leave the world in better shape than you found it. Frederickson also tells us that happiness is something you tap into whenever you feel energized and excited by new ideas, or anytime you feel playful, silly or creative.

Ever hear of the phrase "go with the flow?" Perhaps, as Fredrickson suggests, happiness is similar. Happiness is the ability to lose yourself in something to the point that you don't notice the passage of time. Athletes call this entering "the zone." In fact, many creative people – especially writers – are familiar with this concept. These individuals are so focused and absorbed on the task at hand that they don't notice time passing. For many, this is exactly what enjoying the moment or "being present" is really all about. Could it be that happiness is a self-fulfilling prophecy? If we believe we're happy, we are; the same applies for unhappiness. Happiness is a choice we make every day – sometimes every moment.

What's Your "HQ" – Happiness Quotient?

Now that we've examined some definitions of happiness, the next question to ask ourselves is, "What exactly makes us happy?" We know that happiness is not a static state of mind and that it is something we do not possess at all times (Try as you may to make it so!). Even the happiest of people feel blue at times.

If there were some way to actually measure happiness, like a "happiness quotient" test, perhaps this discussion would not be necessary. You would simply take an "HQ" test – just like an IQ test – and have your results professionally analyzed. Then you would know once and for all if you were happy. Or at the very least, you'd know if you were happy in the moment you took the test! Happiness, though, is difficult to measure, just as it is elusive when you chase it like a butterfly. Why? For one thing, the criteria for happiness are subjective. What makes one person ecstatic may not cause any stir in another.

What if you possessed a "set point" when it comes to happiness? A set point is exactly what it sounds like – one point we keep returning to, regardless of your circumstances. Could your state of happiness be genetically based? You can rule out happiness as an environmental factor. If that were the case, then there would be no sadness in the most beautiful settings of the world. Happiness is also not related to the accumulation of material items. If that were the case, there would be no sad, rich people.

The fact of the matter is that materialism is actually a toxic element to your quest for happiness. "Even rich materialists," according to Ed Diener, a psychologist at the University of Illinois, "aren't as happy as those who care less about getting and receiving." Science can now verify this as well. So what about being happy when you win the lottery? Wouldn't adding a few million to your bank account make you a bit happier? Don't bet on it.

If you're anything like previous lottery winners, you won't be any happier – not for very long at least. In a classic study published in the *Journal of Personality and Social Psychology,* researchers revealed that lottery winners were no happier after they hit it big in winnings than before. Surprisingly, the same study demonstrated that those who suffered with a spinal cord injury "did not appear nearly as unhappy as might be expected." If there were ever two instances that should make one wildly happy for a long, long time or horribly miserable, these two examples might be the ones.

That's why so many psychologists speak of a "set point." It's a certain level of happiness to which you always comfortably settle into. Regardless of the peaks and valleys of emotion in your life, you eventually return to your own personal level of happiness (or unhappiness). This naturally leads to the next question: Can you train your brain to be happy? Maybe so. Some theories now suggest the brain's natural plasticity includes the ability and the capacity to change over time. While this branch of study is relatively new, the results of the research are nothing less than exciting – and in some cases revolutionary. More scientists than ever before say that you can indeed increase the neural networks in your brain in order to cultivate a more positive state of mind.

The most exciting aspect of these theories is the ease with which you can implement them. Don't believe me? You can start right now. Consider the following: You may actually be able to increase neural networks simply and easily by practicing gratitude. Technology now shows that by consciously practicing this simple habit, you may very well achieve higher feelings of reward thanks to neurotransmitters such as dopamine.

As information flows through the brain, neurons fire together in particularly complex ways based upon the information they are representing. In simpler terms, certain regions of the brain can actually stitch together new connections with each other, which is amazing. Think of this "stitching together" as transforming a gravel path into a superhighway of information. That's exactly what you're doing when you continually are thankful for the events and people in your life. Conversely, some researchers now believe that by routinely focusing on the negative aspects of your life, you actually create that superhighway of negative and non-happy thinking.

Chemical Route to Happiness?

No, it's not what you think. I'm not suggesting that you take drugs or illegal chemicals in order to find your personal form of happiness. Did you know there are chemicals you're carrying around right now in your brain which can dramatically increase your happiness? Now that I have your attention, you undoubtedly want to know what these chemicals are.

For starters, let's examine endorphins. Endorphins are neurotransmitters or chemicals in your brain that attach to certain parts of your nervous system. The term "endorphin" came into our vocabulary nearly thirty years ago when they were finally associated with the "runner's high." Perhaps you've heard of this phenomenon. When one runs – or participates in any form of exercise for a specific length of time, the brain releases endorphins. This release provides people with an unquestionable feeling of well-being, and is actually what makes many individuals return to their exercise routine every day. Endorphins, by the way, can be found in all parts of your body.

Another neurotransmitter which plays an important role in happiness is dopamine. Dopamine, unlike endorphins, can be found only in your brain – and specifically in your midbrain. Dopamine helps keep a stressed-out body feeling good. Another feel-good or natural happiness chemical is serotonin. Serotonin is made in the brain, but travels to the blood. If you suffer with depression, it may be due to a low serotonin level. Researchers, though, aren't 100% sure the method by which the body does this. The questions scientists have are actually forms of the old "which came first the chicken or the egg," riddle. They are now searching to discover whether depression lowers serotonin as a side-effect, or if the lack of serotonin causes the depression. In either case, if you can increase your level of serotonin, you just may be able to boost your happiness. But before you run out to find dietary supplements of this substance, consider natural ways of boosting this "happy substance." One of the best ways you'll soon discover is through diet. One of the foods richest in serotonin is turkey.

Your physiology can also help you define your level of happiness. Researchers have been able to measure changes in blood pressure, circulation and heartbeat dependent on your state of happiness. The Institute of HeartMath actually studies varying heart rates. The results? Unhappy individuals tend to have more irregular heartbeats, while those who are happy possess more regular heartbeats. The institute then uses this information to create biofeedback machines that can actually help people develop happier behavior and thought patterns. Having said all of this, maybe we can learn how to be happy after all!

Now that we have examined the brain chemicals that may have an impact on happiness, let's take a look at the difference between happiness and joy. Semantically, people can try to differentiate between the feelings of happiness and joy all day long to little avail. But, ask a biochemist or even a positive psychologist and you may get an entirely different response. That's because the two feelings act on your body differently. It has been theorized that happiness activates the sympathetic nervous system, which stimulates the flight or fight response. Joy, on the other hand, stimulates the parasympathetic nervous system, which controls rest and digestive functions. We weep only from joy or grief whereas we laugh from either joy or happiness.

Without the suffering of captivity or longing, there would be no joy of freedom or reunion, much like the yin versus the yang. Some scientists say that joy is connecting with the source of life within you, while happiness is based more on observing or doing something you really like. Happiness can be fleeting, while joy can be continuous. Joy is self-enabling and comes from within, while happiness is more dependent upon something or someone outside of you.

Many of us need to practice "feeling good" so that we will know what it feels like; we've lost our familiarity with happiness and joy. Like attracts like, so if you want to meet a lot of happy people, you need to find ways to be happier yourself. The more you feel happiness from within, the more that happiness resonates from you and attracts like-minded souls. In a nutshell, happiness comes from the outside while pure joy comes from within.

Defining Happiness for Yourself and Others
How do you define happiness? Is it a way of thinking or is it based on something you will achieve or acquire someday? What would it take for you to be happy in this exact moment in time? Can you

even imagine being happy? What would it look like? What would you look like if you were finally happy?

It has been said that we attract that which we focus on. If this were the case for happiness, then what happens when we focus on the alternative? Focusing on negativity and suffering brings a life devoid of joy and happiness; it is a life focused on the struggle. It is difficult to escape the trap of the struggle, because we often cannot see the forest through the trees. If we would just take a moment to remember all the joys in our lives, perhaps we could begin to turn the situation around. Many times, it is difficult to get out of our own way, because life beats us down.

Looking for Happiness in All the Wrong Places

They say if you can dream it, you can achieve it. Maybe happiness is not really that elusive of a quality after all. Maybe we just need to *decide* to be happy. If you are looking for happiness in all the wrong places, you might just need a shift in perspective. Things and people cannot make us happy, if we are not happy from within. If we have lost our joy for life, then it is up to us to fix it. Maybe it is time to look at happiness as a journey, and not as destination. Happiness is a state of mind.

15

Think back to when you were a child. What were the things that made you happy? Maybe they weren't things at all. Happiness for me was spending time with people I loved like my grandfather and grandmother. My grandfather used to take us for day trips in his old Model A antique car where he would pack a lunch and show us how to skip rocks. That was happiness. We used to take a yearly vacation in Ft. Lauderdale, Florida, where we would sit out on the sea wall at night and just listen to the waves crashing in on the shore, enjoying the company of good family and friends. That was happiness. Growing up, my mother used to take us every week to this old candy store that had fake dummies sitting in rocking chairs on the front porch. The candy store had every kind of candy that you could imagine, from wax lips to Pixy Stix to colorful buttons on a strip of paper. That was happiness.

Sometimes our memories are happier than the event itself, and maybe that's good. Maybe that is nature's way of helping us focus on the good things in life. Time eases our pain, but it also enhances our memories. Think about all of the wonderful experiences you have had in your life up to this point in time, and take a moment to remember and reflect on them now, just for a little while.

Steps to Action: Chapter One

- Don't wait for "Happiness" to come knocking on your door.
- Decide to be happy today, for today is all we really have and tomorrow never comes.
- Figure out if you have a "happiness set point" by visiting Dr. Martin Seligman's Authentic Happiness page and taking the Authentic Happiness Inventory Questionnaire at http://www.authentichappiness.sas.upenn.edu/
- Visit the Institute of Heart Math at http://www.heartmath.org/ and learn how to lower your stress and build resilience.
- Practice feeling good for a change.
- Figure out how YOU define happiness.
- Focus on the positive in each and every situation, for thoughts become reality. For example, practice the act of gratitude so that your brain can construct a superhighway of information to help spread the feeling of happiness.
- Discover ways in which you can boost the levels of three happiness chemicals naturally found in your system: endorphins, dopamine, and serotonin.
- Research the possibility of using a form of biofeedback to aid in boosting your "happiness quotient."

Chapter Two: Happiness: The Journey

There once was a wise person who quietly instructed us to take time to smell the roses.

No one really needs to be told what that means. And probably no one would even argue with the advice. So why aren't more of us actually following this bit of wisdom? Are you so focused on where you are going that you are missing the sights along the way? You're not alone. Sometimes, the joy lies in the discovery of each and every happy moment – in smelling each individual rose. Many times, the trip is more fun than the actual destination.

Think back to when you were a child getting ready for a vacation. Especially, think about a vacation that meant you were traveling a long distance. Remember the fun in merely anticipating the trip. As a youngster, I always looked forward to our family road trip. We would spend hours packing the car, putting pillows and blankets in and making sure we had plenty of snacks to occupy our time and fill our bellies. Along the way, my father would point out sights for us to look at. We played travel bingo to occupy our time. There was even a time, believe it or not, when the highway didn't go all the way through to Florida, which forced us to explore the lazy back roads of Georgia, where we would stop at all the wonderful peach stands on our way down south.

What does this have to do with happiness? My happiness existed in the trip, not the destination. My family enjoyed many happy moments along the way. In turn, they are some of my most treasured memories. I don't remember the actual vacation destinations as much as I remember the fun we all had along the way, sharing memories and moments. Life – and especially happiness – is a lot like this. The beauty doesn't lie in the final point of success, but in the time it took to get you there and the people you met along the way. Hopefully, you've met many wonderful people along your road of life and you have had your own excellent and exciting adventures. If you can't recount any great adventures, it's time to start enjoying the moment more. After all, you only get one shot at this thing called life, and the moment is fleeting.

Something to do, something to love, and something to hope for. These three "somethings," according to Allan K. Chambers, are the grand essentials of happiness. Want others to be happy? The Dalai Lama says it's only possible if we practice compassion. Want happiness for yourself? Then you must do the same. Samuel Johnson said that hope is itself a species of happiness, and perhaps the chief happiness which this world affords.

Of Course, You Deserve True Happiness!

Do you feel, like many others, that you don't "deserve" happiness? I see people each and every day who are simply beaten down by life. Yes, life can be very challenging, but we all deserve to be happy. It's your *right* to be happy, plain and simple. Remember what it says in the Declaration of Independence; while I may quibble with the phrase "pursuit of happiness," there's no doubt you deserve it. We all deserve amazing lives.

You can find happiness simply by giving something away. It's true. By doing one simple act of kindness, you'll feel amazingly happier. That's according to research conducted by Martin Seligman, who sent college students off on a quest. He gave two groups a five dollar bill and instructed one group to buy something for themselves. He told the other group to buy something for someone else. When they returned, those who gave their five dollars away in some form – whether the money or something that money could buy – felt better than those who spent it on themselves.

Can't afford to give anyone a material present? That doesn't matter. Why not give someone your time or even a hug? We could all use a little more of that. Remember, happiness comes from within, so if you don't feel like you deserve it, no one can give it to you. But more importantly, you can't spread it around if you don't have it yourself. Take some time to appreciate yourself for the magnificent being that you are, no matter what your circumstances. Then, take a little more time to share the happiness.

Does Your Happiness Depend on Something?

What is your happiness dependent on? If your answer was someone other than yourself, then you may be in trouble. Hopefully, you saw this one coming. You may have already realized that no one can make you happy except for yourself.

Let's face it. Your circumstances are always changing. That's why so many lottery winners fail to find that end-all happiness that they believed was waiting at the end of the rainbow. Think you can entrust your happiness to someone else – your parents, your spouse, your children? Eventually people let us down. This is partly because it is too much pressure continually trying to make someone happy and also because it's not their "job" to make you happy. They're concentrating on their own happiness.

21

There are many people out there who simply get caught up looking for happiness in everyone but themselves. Many of us are not happy with who we are at the deepest levels of our existence, and that is truly a shame. People don't complete us, contrary to what you might think. Companionship and love are wonderful–don't get me wrong–but each partner must bring his or her own happiness and joy to the table, or the equation is unbalanced. If your happiness is dependent on someone else, it's time to shift the load and take back responsibility for your own well-being and happiness. Believe me, not only will the person you've been depending on for this appreciate it, but so will you. No one can make you shine if you don't *shine from within*. That's all there is to it.

A Thousand Tiny Moments in Which We Can Be Happy

Take a look at life from this perspective: life, indeed, is made up of thousands of small, passing moments in which we can choose – or not choose – to be happy. This means that we have an infinite number of single moments of choice. Happiness is never out of reach, because its potential is available to us in every single second.

Take a moment now to think about the things that really make you happy. What if you could experience one of those moments right now? What would you be doing? What would you look like? Who would you be with? What if there were a magical island you could go to where everyone was happy? Hard to imagine, isn't it? Think about your perfect day right now and imagine what it would look like. Would you go walking in the rain, just to feel the gentle drops? Would you take a moment to just sit down and enjoy life? Would you bake some cookies or make an aromatic cup of coffee, just so you could smell the joy?

What if you could sit on the beach and sink your toes into the sand for just a moment, enjoying the warm sun? What if you could take a long nap, on a warm, lazy summer day? What if you could step out of life, for just a moment, and let some love in? Just imagine yourself taking time out of your day to go get a massage and have a cup of tea. How about taking yourself on a wonderful vacation in your mind where you sit at a beautiful café in Paris, watching the world go by?

These are the moments which make up our lives, and we can experience them right here, right now if we choose to. The imagination is a very powerful tool, and it can take us places that no one can else can. The imagination isn't limited by the normal barriers of space and time; you don't need any special talents to arrive at any of these magical places. All you need to do is close your eyes, take a deep breath, and picture yourself there, just enjoying the moment.

When was the last time you simply enjoyed a singular moment? Does this remind you of the adage, "Life happens while you're making other plans?" It is important to take the time to smell the roses because those roses give us hope. As corny as it sounds, it's true: the best things in life are free, because money is not really what makes us happy.

Try a simple exercise now. Sit down and get comfortable, and take a deep breath. Imagine that there is a beautiful light shining over your head. Imagine this light filling your body. Take another couple of deep breaths, and see what images come into your mind. Do you see a beautiful mountain range or are you by the sea? Maybe you're taking a long voyage on a wonderful train, or traveling by sea on a beautiful ship. Perhaps you are wrapped up in a warm blanket, sitting by a beautiful fire. If you're more the adventurous type, maybe you have traveled back in time and are you enjoying a soak in a beautiful old Roman Bath, with someone taking care of your every need. Wherever you may be, just take a moment now to drink in the quiet and see and feel every little detail.

Now that you're completely relaxed, I want to ask you a question. What if you woke up tomorrow and suddenly had everything you have always dreamed about? What if all of your problems were suddenly solved? What would be different? Imagine with me, for a moment, that a miracle has happened, and you have suddenly gotten everything you have always wanted. How would you spend your days? How would you contribute and make the world a better place? Imagine with me that you have the freedom and flexibility to pursue your dreams. What is your number one passion? Take this moment to imagine what your life would be like without all your problems.

We all come to this earth with a gift. What is yours? There are hundreds, if not thousands of ways to make a difference; how would you make a difference? What if you could turn that very thing that you have always struggled with into something that you could teach the world about?

"Perhaps all the dragons of our lives are princesses who are only waiting to see us once beautiful and brave." - Rainer Maria Rilke

Steps to Action: Chapter Two

- Start learning to enjoy the journey and the sights along the way on your road to happiness.

- Practice spreading love and compassion by taking time to visit someone less fortunate than you.

- Decide how important happiness is to you, and make it a priority in your life.

- Learn how to shine from *within*. Don't allow someone else to control your happiness.

- Try our simple relaxation exercise, and ask yourself the miracle question: "What if I woke up tomorrow and suddenly had everything I had always dreamed about?" How would your life be different?

- Make a list of the thousand tiny moments in which you can be happy.

Chapter Three: The Road to Recovery

Why Am I Not Happy?

What would it take for you to be happy? In order to answer this question, you must first ask yourself how happy your mindset is. What's the message you are sending the world? Is it a positive one, or a negative one? Don't think for a moment; I'm asking these questions lightly. However, you may be amazed at exactly how much this influences your life. Your mindset consists of the song you sing, and the dance you dance. It is a sum of all the energy you emanate into the world. If your mindset is a positive one, congratulations! If it isn't, you're probably well aware of it. You're presumably living the happiest life possible.

"All the world is a stage," Shakespeare famously said. If that's true, then your mindset could be considered our theatre with you playing the leading role. Perhaps your play has been on Broadway so long that you're reciting your lines by rote. By just "going through the motions" of life, you are used to acting and thinking a certain way. As a consequence, you don't pay much attention to how much your mindset has an influence over your life. Each and every one of us is emitting energy of one kind or another. After all, everything is energy, from the smallest drop of water to the largest tree. Yes, you are energy as well. Science tells us that energy can neither be created nor destroyed; it can only be transformed. If your energy isn't working on your behalf in a positive fashion, you may be short-changing yourself.

If you were asked right now to create your own eulogy, what you would say? Would you be proud of all your accomplishments? Would you be proud of the people you helped each step of the way, or the lives you've touched? Looking back, have you had a happy life or did you spend your life struggling? If you can't recall having a happy, fulfilled life, don't give up hope. It's never too late to turn back the clock and make it right. If there's something you wish you had done, but never quite had the time to, the time is *now*. If you're not living your best life, then right here, right *now* is the perfect time to learn how to change your mindset.

As we discussed earlier, happiness is a state of mind. Happiness is a decision you must consciously make. We all take time to maintain our bodies every day. We take time to eat right and exercise; we take time out to go to the doctor if we are not feeling well. Most of us, though, are not doing much to improve our state of mind, and we suffer because of it. The beautiful thing about a mindset is that it can be changed instantaneously. There are many ways you can go about doing this. You can do affirmations, engage in various self-improvement activities such as meditation or yoga, take a run to clear out the cobwebs, or you could even be hypnotized. It doesn't really matter which road you choose, as long as you choose to do something.

The easiest way to elicit change is to give your mind suggestions that reflect the life you *want to be living*. Your life is simply a reflection of that which you program into your mind. If you don't like what your mind has manifested for you, then maybe it's time to do something about it.

Thoughts Become Things -- What Are You Thinking?

Perhaps Ralph Waldo Emerson said it best: "A man is what he thinks about all day long." The truth of the matter is that thoughts really do become reality. It's now time to ask your mind what it has been thinking all this time. As a matter of fact, you really don't have to ask at all; just look around your life and see what you find. Your life will tell you what you have been thinking because your thoughts manifest your particular reality in each and every moment of each and every day.

Never, ever underestimate the power of expectation. Expectation often means the difference between failure and success. If you don't feel like your life is ever going to change and you are sitting around waiting for some magical moment, then I have news for you: you have to make your own moment, starting now. Life is not a spectator sport; if you want your life to change, then you have to take steps to improve it. Once you begin thinking in terms of expectation and exhilaration, you begin to draw good things and good people into your life. Much like the principle of *like attracts like*, your mind simply follows whatever you have programmed into it. Still, you must have faith in order to achieve success.

Changing Your Thought Processes Going Forward

Believe it or not, it took you years to develop your particular mindset. Don't assume you can change overnight. Changing your attitude may not be an easy process, but that's not to say it's impossible. Not by any stretch of the imagination.

Much like a fine work of art that's never quite complete, taking small steps to improve your mindset works, but the changes you bring about may be subtle at first. If you were able to closely examine Michelangelo's work in the Sistine Chapel, you would see that this gorgeous work of art is actually made up of a countless number of separate brush strokes that wouldn't look like much if each were viewed individually. However, we all know the work is magnificent when viewed from afar. It took Michelangelo many moons to complete his work, just like it will take you. Your mindset and your attitude should be something you are always working on in some way, shape, or form. The point is not to finish, but to enjoy the work along the way.

Can You Really Attract Happiness?

At the beginning, we compared happiness to that elusive butterfly that remained just out of reach. Regardless of how fast you chased it, you couldn't quite grasp it. So, can you really attract happiness? And if you can, how in the world do you go about doing it?

Is your happiness dependent on *circumstances* or *perception*? It is well-noted that if you want to attract more friends, then you must learn to be a friend first. The same analogy can be used for happiness. If you want to attract happy people into your life, you must first learn how to be happy on your own. Likewise, negative people attract other negative people, and you can feel their energy coming a mile away. Positive people have a way of drawing other positive people (and things) to them like a magnet.

There are two ways in which most people view the world, and our attitudes and our perception can literally shape the world around us. You are either the type of person who sees the glass as half empty or the type of person that sees the glass as half full. Take a moment to stop and figure out right now which kind of person you are. Which attitude is more prevalent in your life? There is something to be said about having a positive attitude, because our attitudes spill out and infect everyone around us.

People with negative attitudes are "energy vampires." They can actually suck the positive energy right out of you – before you even know it's happening. They're no fun to be around. While everyone is entitled to a bad day every once in a while, those who constantly view the world as a "bad" place or see the cup as half empty, often attract the same kind of energy right back to them – the "hopeless" kind of energy. It's difficult to maintain a positive attitude when you're around negative people most of the time. The minute our positive attitude is lost, our luck changes and we begin to attract the same kind of negative energy right back into our surroundings.

It's not easy breaking out of a pattern because our habits are like comfortable, old blankets we have just gotten used to. Just think back to a February morning, when the snow was falling gently and the temperature outside was about 20 degrees. Did you really want to get out of bed? When that alarm rang what was your first instinct – to jump out of bed enthusiastically or to curl up under that blanket and remain in your very real "comfort zone?"

Many people can look at the events that have occurred in their lives and recognize the patterns. Most of us spend a lot of time and energy repeating the same old destructive ones, over and over again. Why? Simply because we haven't instructed our minds or our brains to do otherwise.

Is Happiness Dependent on Circumstances or Perception?

The road to your "happiness recovery" and a renewed, reinvigorated life requires an emotional shift. While this is no small feat, it is something you're capable of accomplishing. This shift will challenge your current conditioning—the conditioning that tells you that in order to have a happy life, you must wait for your external conditions or circumstances to change.

While not everyone has the same opportunities in terms of material wealth, we all share the same opportunities to be happy. Remember, your happiness is not dependent on external circumstances. This can't be said often enough. To put this another way, your peace of mind or your ability to laugh is certainly not dependent on what's happening around you – or it shouldn't be. Perhaps your problems or your comforts may be dependent upon external circumstances, but your inner peace and your inner state of mind comes from within.

Here's another statement that may come as a revelation to you: Your suffering is not actually caused by the situations you find yourself in. What brings on suffering – or joy – for that matter, lies in the meanings you attribute to them. Your mind is a great storyteller. It tells you a story and you believe each and every word like it is gospel.

Our society has conditioned us to accept disappointment and to accommodate distress. When you're suffering, you are most likely told that suffering is part of the human existence. After all, someone probably advised you at some time that life is not a bowl full of cherries. Instead, we're taught to roll with the punches of life. After all, it is a stormy sea. We struggle to make a living; we struggle to maintain relationships; we struggle to maintain our health, and we even struggle for survival.

We know how to struggle, but do we know to *live*? The bigger question is: Why must you accept this viewpoint? Why can't you live an extraordinary life? Of course, you can. Your first step is to challenge this conditioning. You must learn to outwit it, once and for all; your happiness depends upon it.

Steps to Action: Chapter Three
- Ask yourself if your energy–or mindset–is working for you or against you.
- Make a list of suggestions that reflect the life you want to be living, and take a few minutes each day to focus in on them.
- Practice writing your own eulogy, so you can honestly see if you have lived the life you want to be living.
- Ask yourself if you are an optimist or a pessimist, and be honest. Then think about how this may be affecting your chances of feeling happy.
- Make a seismic emotional shift by challenging your old conditioning and thought processes.

Chapter Four: The Risks of Being a People Pleaser

The Oxygen Mask Analogy

If you haven't heard the "oxygen mask analogy," here goes:

If you are on an airplane with your child and the pressure in the cabin suddenly drops, you are well advised to first put your own oxygen mask on before placing a mask on your child. The reasoning lies in the fact that you won't be much good to your child if you happen to pass out before you get a chance to put their oxygen mask on. It's important to remember to always put yourself first, because you aren't much good to those around you and those you love, if you're falling apart at the seams.

People love taking care of other people, but to do so at your own expense turns you into something called a "people pleaser." While others may find this pleasurable, if you engage in this behavior long enough and neglect your own pleasures, it can be detrimental to your happiness and your self-esteem. Simply put, you cannot make everyone happy, so what is the point in trying? Face it: we're all people pleasers to some extent. Some individuals simply don't know when to stop. You can either go around emotionally deprived while trying to incessantly please others, or you can spend your time living and creating your own authentic life, fine-tuned to your own needs and desires.

How does someone get started on this road to people-pleasing anyway? For some, it starts in childhood; for others it may not become apparent until adulthood. While it's good to be a pleasing, agreeable person, it definitely is not good to create a pattern of living that allows others to be manipulative or insensitive towards you. There are four requirements that people pleasers often impose upon themselves which ultimately contribute to their emotional and relational discord. First, they often run interference and find themselves taking on responsibility for others' moods. In other words, they take on responsibility for what is not theirs. They continue to carry this action to the extent that they do whatever it takes in order to minimize what others are responsible for.

People pleasers can also be enablers. In this way, they allow others' bad habits and attitudes to continue. Often, they rationalize this behavior by denying what is healthy and by playing into improper relationship patterns.

Consider the following characteristics of people pleasers:

- People pleasers may play into the self-serving schemes of others either wittingly or unwittingly.
- People pleasers may allow false guilt or fear to be a primary motivator for behavior.
- People pleasers suppress their emotions.
- People pleasers may try to take responsibility for others' happiness—or even others' distress.
- People pleasers often live with the feeling of walking on eggshells when it comes to another's feelings.
- People pleasers have trouble standing up for their own convictions.
- People pleasers may subconsciously encourage others to take advantage of them in disrespect.
- People pleasers become appeasers when others get angry and, often times, their direction is actually based upon the actions of others.

Why Happiness Should Come from Within

Do any of these behaviors sound familiar to you? Recognizing once and for all how these people-pleasing behaviors rule your life frees you to opt out of the excessively compliant role you may have placed yourself in. Your happiness should come from within and it shouldn't be dependent on someone else's behavior.

According to Jonathan Haidt, mentioned previously as the author of *The Happiness Hypothesis*, our brain inherits a set point for an average level of happiness. While some people have a naturally high set point–meaning that they come by happiness easily–others do not. This does not mean, however, that these individuals are doomed to live forever at this specific set point. If you're one of those whose set point isn't exactly where you would like it to be, you can choose to change it. While many factors may move your set point up or down, it is important to know what your set point is, so that you can take steps to overcome it if it is not at the level you desire.

There are ways you can improve your happiness set point. Some of these include practicing meditation, exercising, and even hypnotherapy or self-hypnosis. Meditation is actually one of the oldest and most widely used mental hygiene techniques in the world and hypnosis is real, even though its exact mechanisms are not well understood. Some other areas in which you can improve include improving your relationships by having a few people in your life that you care about, improving your work, and improving your connection to something beyond yourself, whatever that may be.

Happiness and Relationships

What about happiness and relationships? Do relationships affect our happiness? If so, how? Relationships have a huge effect on your life. When they are great your world is wonderful. When they are bad, it feels as if your world is crumbling.

Try asking yourself the deathbed question: On your deathbed, will you wish you had spent more time at the office, or with your friends and family? I hope you answered friends and family! While happiness is important within the context of a relationship, it shouldn't be the only thing that makes you happy. Relationships must be nurtured and enjoyed, but it's important for each party to bring their own happiness to the table, for we must support each other during the ups and downs, which inevitably occur. Perhaps you learned early in life that other people determine your happiness. This is such a deep-set belief that it stays with us for a lifetime. You may look for happiness in everything and everyone except yourself. Remember the people pleaser?

Deep down, you may fear being alone. This fear may drive you to make poor decisions in your relationships and your behavior. What happens if in the process of discovering your own happiness that you discover there are people around you bringing you down?

Cleaning House and Getting Rid of the Naysayers

It's hard to make room for new things or new people in your life when there are things (or people) weighing you down. It's been said that in order to make room for new things, you must first purge the old. It's my philosophy that this applies to people as well as things, because sometimes the people in our lives drag us down. If we are to expect new, great things to come into our lives, then we must first get rid of the old things that are holding us back.

Of course, this is much easier said than done. Many of us get very attached not only to the things that we have but to our relationships as well. Even if they aren't healthy for us or they're no longer serving a useful purpose, we may still feel compelled to hold on to them. Sometimes, we simply outgrow the people or relationships in our lives, plain and simple.

People who don't support your way of thinking can deplete you of everything that is good in your life and in your thoughts. It may not have started out that way, but for some of us, it ends up that way. If there is someone in your life dragging you down, maybe it's time to take a closer look at the situation to see if the dynamic can be changed. Sometimes people – even good friends – just grow and change at different rates. That's not only normal, but to be expected. It may be that some relationships were only meant to last for a certain reason or a certain season in our lives. If you find yourself in a situation or relationship you have outgrown, maybe it is time to take back your power.

Taking Back Your Power

It may seem at times that your life simply spins out of control because of extenuating circumstances; other times, you may have simply given up hope. It's never too late to take back your power and regain control over your life. In the end, you need to be able to admit that your choices have brought you to the place you are today. It's really that simple. Relationships are meant to comfort and provide a shelter from the storm. If yours is no longer doing that, it might be time to stand up and take your place in the sun. Life was meant to be lived with joy, not merely tolerated.

None of us make good choices all the time. At one time or another, we all find ourselves regretting some choice. Even though you may think you have made some seemingly questionable choices, it doesn't really matter. You read that right. It does you no good to sit around and ponder or even bemoan your past mistakes. You can't change history. All you really have control over are the decisions you make from this point forward. In other words, you can take control of your life and of your happiness. If your life is not making you happy, you can change it. If you don't change it, no one else will.

So many of us spend so much time walking around on eggshells trying to make other people happy and proud of us, that we lose sight of the most important person in our lives, namely ourselves. You cannot be a good mother, a great father or even a wonderful best friend, if you're not happy in your own right. Even though it may be painful examining the broken relationships in your life, it's sometimes necessary. As the saying goes, with pain comes power and with power comes happiness.

Steps to Action: Chapter Four
- Ask yourself if you think you could be a people pleaser. Look over this checklist and see if any of these behaviors sound familiar:
  - It tends to bother me if I have upset someone.

- o I usually feel that I try harder than others do to make relationships work.
- o People would be surprised if they were aware of the resentment that I have bottled up.
- o When I do something for my own pleasure, I feel selfish.
- o I have to tread lightly due to key people who are moody.
- o Sometimes I just try too hard to be nice.
- o I have remained in bad or toxic relationships for much longer than I should have.
- o It seems that other people will only accept me as long as I conform to the way they do things.
- Take steps to improve your happiness set point by learning meditation or engage in some other kind of self-reflective activity to improve your mental hygiene.
- Clean your emotional house and take stock of those people around you who may be bringing you down.
- Take back your power by releasing the past and changing the decisions you make going forward.

Chapter Five: Developing a Happiness Mindset

Finding Happiness in an Unhappy World

How do you find happiness in an unhappy and frustrating world? Life can be challenging at best, even for the happiest amongst us. How can you harness the power of emotion to increase your chances of happiness? The world can be a difficult place at times, and we all face challenges in our lives on a daily basis. We all experience highs and lows, good times and bad times. That's just life. However, if you are experiencing more bad times than good, maybe it is time to figure out what you can do about it.

Steps You Can Take to Improve Your Life Now

Let's talk about some of the things you can do *right now* to improve your life. These activities may seem silly or trivial, but sometimes it's the little things we do that make the biggest difference. Sometimes our minds have an emotional "tipping point" and we just get used to thinking or acting a certain way. Some people call this a comfort zone. It's easier to stay miserable in your comfort zone, than to take a chance on leaving it. Once you leave it, you really don't know what you may encounter.

By taking an active role in your mental health, you'll be on the path to healing.

- Try making a list of those activities that you really enjoy doing.
- Think of those things that make you happy while you're doing them.
- List some activities you would like to try in the future and schedule those activities on a regular basis.
- Remember to socialize often; we tend to spend too much time focusing on the stressors in life. Spending time with friends can help us get our mind off of certain stressors, which will help us in the long run.
- Try volunteering.
- Get more quality sleep.
- Avoid doing unpleasant things if you can.
- Try rating your overall happiness on a scale from 1-10 on a daily basis, and see what you average!

Yin Versus Yang – Can There Be Happiness Without Suffering?

Black versus white, yin versus yang, happiness versus suffering–that is the question. How would we know the beauty of one, without the pain of the other? Absence makes the heart grow fonder, so they say, but is it really true? There's great suffering in the world, but there are also great stories of hope. Life is bittersweet, but maybe that's OK. Happiness without sadness would not be complete as long as the suffering persists. We need to experience all feelings and emotions, including sadness and suffering, because it makes us appreciate life more. People often try and move away from feelings of sadness as quickly as possible.

If you tend to do this, think about this question for a moment. What if, instead of moving away from the feelings of sadness, you took steps to feel empowered by them? Can sadness really empower us, if our heart is broken into a million pieces? You may be surprised by the answer. You can't escape suffering, as it is simply part of the human condition. Suffering is a fundamental characteristic of the way in which we lead our lives. For far too many of us, happiness is fleeting – like the elusive butterfly. Why? Most people instantly respond, "Because life gets in the way." We are rarely satisfied for more than a moment. Before we know it, we are onto the next goal, the next experience, or the next possession.

What if we allowed sadness to let a spark into our lives instead? What if sadness actually helped us open up our heart, by giving us the courage to touch our own pain and suffering? It has been said that suffering is the common thread that unites all of humanity. Recognizing this sense of interconnection has the possibility to bring about unspeakable joy, *if we allow it to*.

Everyone encounters some degree of sadness in their lives. Change – and sometimes sadness – is inevitable. Change is the only constant in life, so it's only logical that until we learn how to change gracefully, we will continue to suffer. The presence of sadness in our lives makes us realize that there is impermanence all around us. However, sadness can also help us realize the blessing of each and every precious moment in life in a far more satisfying and fulfilling way. Times of great grief can also lead to times of great joy and love, because they give us perspective. Opening your heart to love also opens it to pain, but that may not always be a bad thing.

The Silver Lining – How to Turn a Bad Situation Around

You've heard the saying "every cloud has a silver lining," but is it really true? No doubt you've been in a position at some point in which you thought that there couldn't possibly be a silver lining! Do silver linings just miraculously appear or do you have to do something to reach them?

It's not fun to fail, but if you're planning on doing anything important in your life, failure is a necessary step. There is no success without some failures along the way. There's no shame in failing; it just depends on what you can learn from it. Embarrassment, frustration, failure, and bad situations are a part of life. Listed below are some practical steps you can take to move past failure:

- Find meaning by asking yourself how you can use the experience to grow.
- Keep a failure log, because it helps you focus more on growth and learning.
- Find a new goal and don't dwell in the past. Get out of the rut and start building momentum again.
- Remove chronic sources of stress by keeping your energy high and letting go of people in your life who are a source of negativity; find outlets for stress.
- Build a support base.
- Be humble and have a sense of humor.
- Stop analyzing and start doing something new.

Finding meaning is important because it helps you learn, change, and grow. Viktor Frankl even found meaning while suffering in a Nazi concentration camp. If he could find meaning through such a horrific experience, you can find meaning in your life. It is important to ask yourself what the experience has taught you. Perhaps the experience has made you stronger, wiser, or even kinder.

This suggestion may sound a little off the wall, but keep an open mind. Why not a failure log? I know the last thing you want to do is to remind yourself of the times you've failed, but this is a beautiful way in which to learn from those mistakes. Writing them down – admitting them, in effect – makes you more willing to take chances when the only risk to you is your pride. Some people even learn to laugh at their failures, telling themselves that if they don't have a few major failures a year then perhaps they aren't trying hard enough! That's not mere rationalization; it's the truth.

Finding a new goal helps keep you from dwelling too much in the past and helps you focus on something positive. A new goal can also help you focus more on the new opportunities, instead of dwelling on a current stumble. Stress can also play havoc when it comes to your happiness, so it's important to keep your energy high by staying in good shape and disassociating yourself from people who may be a source of negativity. Moreover, finding outlets for your stress will help you recover. Building a support system of friends and colleagues will help you keep your head held high when times get rough. Having a sense of humor goes a long way in helping us stay humble and in moving us forward when times are difficult.

The most important step you can take, however, is to stop analyzing yourself and start doing something new! There's a limit to how much learning you can actually gain from an experience. Sometimes we try to learn too much from an experience and end up beating our heads against the wall to no avail. Learn what you can, and learn what you need. But most importantly, learn to move on.

Finding Your Passion and Purpose

If you do what you love, you will *never work a day in your life*. Some of the most successful people in the world are living by this principle, and, there's good reason for it. Doing what you love makes your world shine. Finding your passion and purpose is critical to success. Have you ever loved doing something so much, that you have gotten lost in time? Have you ever started something and looked up five minutes later, only to discover it's five hours later? Have you ever forgotten to eat because you simply lost track of time? I have and you can too.

Everyone has a gift; you just have to figure out what yours is. Find something you love, and go do it.

What is your true calling in life? If you haven't figured it out yet, there's still time (there's always time!). Below are seven questions you can ask yourself to help discover if you are living your true passion.

- Do you get excited by the things you do every day?
- Do others comment on how happy you are and what fun you are to be around?
- Do you get upset and thrown off track when unexpected circumstances and situations occur?
- Are you clear about the top five passions in your life, or those things that matter to you the most?
- Do you spend time doing the things you love surrounded by the people you love?
- Is life confusing to you, or do you lack a clear sense of direction?

The answers to these questions should help you reveal whether you're living your passion. If you don't get excited and turned on by the things you do every day, then what does excite you? People who are living their passion are on fire for all the world to see. Their confidence and commitment shows because they are truly happy doing what they love. Doing anything else is simply drudgery. I guarantee there is something you do better than anyone else on earth. Just as no two snowflakes are ever alike, no two people are ever alike in terms of the gifts they bring to this world. When you see a person who has something you want, it is important to move beyond envy and resentment and let him enjoy his success. Instead of feeling jealousy, his good fortune should give you hope that you can achieve the same level for yourself.

Sometimes pursuing your passion takes great courage and faith, for the road is difficult. When you are called to service, you're simply compelled to share your gift with the world. You'll do anything to get there. It's not easy chasing a dream, but the prize at the end is worth it, for you never have to work another day in your life. Maybe that's the real meaning of happiness. Do what you love, and the world will be your oyster.

Steps to Action: Chapter Five
- Take steps to improve your life today:
  - Make a list of those things that make you happy.
  - Socialize often and spend more time with friends.

- o Volunteer.
- o Get more sleep.
- o Avoid doing unpleasant things if you can.
- o Rate your overall happiness on a scale from 1-10 every day.
- Learn how to embrace change.
- Try to find the silver lining and learn to turn a bad situation around.
- Discover your passion and purpose in life by figuring out what you love to do beyond anything else.

Chapter Six: Happiness is a Decision

The Train Trip

We've examined happiness as a journey before, but now let's examine happiness as a decision that you must consciously make. You – and you alone – have the ultimate say when it comes to your happiness, whether you believe it or not. Consider the following analogy of a train trip:

There once was a young man who was looking forward to going on a trip. He couldn't wait to reach his destination, and he was planning on taking a train to get there. He had planned this trip for a very long time. He had clothes for every day of the week and an exhausting itinerary. He told everyone about his upcoming trip to Timbuktu, and the time finally arrived for him to leave after many long months of waiting. As the man boarded the train, he noticed many happy people, and he wondered why they were so happy.

A few hours into the trip, the train hit a snag and broke down in the middle of nowhere. Despite this, everyone still seemed very happy except for the young man, who was annoyed at the delay. He stormed up to the conductor and asked what was going on, and was told that they were doing the best they possibly could; it would be several hours, if not a day, before they could get going again.

The young man was highly agitated and couldn't believe his luck to be stuck on a dismal train with a bunch of strangers. Deciding to try and make the best out of a bad situation, he decided to go out into the train to see if he could get something to eat. He sat down at one of the small tables and attempted to enjoy some peace and quiet and a cup of tea. The man wasn't alone for long before an old man came up to sit with him. The old man looked tired, so he thought it wouldn't hurt to make some pleasant conversation. He asked the man how long he had been on the train. The old man laughed and replied, "I have been on this train for a very long time, that's all you really need to know."

The young man found this strange, but proceeded to talk to the kind man anyway. Hours went by and much conversation took place. The young man learned much from the wise old sage, and he was happy he took the time to meet him. Several more hours passed, but the train had yet to move. The young man met many more interesting and intriguing people and heard many lovely stories about life along the way. Still, he was still a little annoyed that the train had not yet moved. He continued to meet many interesting characters on the train,

56

including a magician, a funeral director, an actor, and a lovely young woman. More time passed until it was finally the next day, and everyone was still in good spirits, which was hard to believe.

The young man, although deterred, realized there wasn't much that could be done so he decided to start enjoying the journey. Before he knew it, the train was moving and he was speeding along to his destination. He was now almost two days late which cut his trip short, being that he was only planning on being gone for five. He was sad to say goodbye to all his wonderful new friends, but he had to go because he had an important destination to get to. When the young man finally arrived at his destination, he couldn't believe what he saw. The village was deserted. Not knowing what to do, he decided to start walking to see what he could find.

Amazingly enough, he found more interesting and intriguing people along the way that offered to share their travel adventures with him. The young man was perplexed that he had such a good time, because he never really got to his original destination. Surprisingly, the same thing happened on his way home, and he was delayed another extra two days trying to get back home.

When the young man arrived home, everyone asked him how his trip was, and he replied, "Quite interesting." As he proceeded to tell about his adventures while trying to get to Timbuktu, his grandfather laughed, because it turned out he had intentionally planned all the delays and mishaps. When the truth finally came out, the young man asked his grandfather why he would do such a thing. The grandfather replied that he did it because the young man was missing out on life. He was always focused on the destination rather than the journey, and he didn't want his grandson to end up like he did, regretting all of the time he had spent waiting to get somewhere and missing the journey along the way.

Cooking Up Happiness: What's Your Personal Recipe?

What's your personal recipe for happiness? Everyone has a unique combination all their own. Everyone wants to be happy. Some find it easy, while others seemingly search forever. Sometimes happiness is right there in front of our nose, and we just don't realize it. Some people think money makes them happy, but that is a misguided reality. Having nice things is great, but it doesn't really make you happy in the long run. I ran across a simple recipe for happiness that I would like to share:

2 Heaping cups of patience

1 Heart full of love

2 Hands full of generosity

A dash of laughter

1 Head full of understanding

Sprinkle generously with kindness, add plenty of faith and mix well.

Spread over a period of a lifetime and serve everyone you meet.

~Author unknown~

Sharing the Love: The Pink Bubble Technique

Now I'm sure you are wondering what the pink bubble technique is. The pink bubble is both a meditation technique and a way to spread good thoughts and feelings to someone. If you encounter someone with negative energy, you can send them a pink bubble to help them work through their negative belief system. You may be amazed at how effective this little technique really is. Our minds are incredible tools that many of us simply don't use to their full level of effectiveness. If you run across someone who is having a bad day, try sending them a pink bubble full of happy thoughts and see if it makes a difference in their mood or their state of mind!

You can also use this technique as a quick meditation to help you relax, or to help you manifest things you may need or want. The best part about this meditation is that it is surprisingly simple and quite effective.

Exercise the following to manifest something:

- Lie or sit down in a comfortable position, close your eyes and breathe slowly, deeply, and naturally. Relax yourself gradually and start feeling this meditation taking you deeper and deeper into a state of relaxation.
- To manifest something, imagine a specific thing or situation that you would like to manifest. Imagine that it already has occurred.
- Picture what you would like to manifest as clearly as possible in your mind. Take the fantasy you presently see in your mind's eye and surround it with a pink bubble. Now, place your goal inside of that bubble. Why is the bubble pink? The color associated with the heart is pink. Having this color-vibration surrounding what you want to manifest will bring to you only that which is in perfect affinity with your being.
- The next step is to let go of it. Imagine the bubble is now floating up and into the

universe, with your vision still contained within it. This symbolically shows that you are emotionally "letting go" of your manifestation.

- Now your manifestation is free to float around in the universe, gathering and attracting energy for its future manifestation.
- That's all there is to it.

Exercise to send someone love:

- Lie or sit down in a comfortable position, close your eyes and breathe slowly, deeply, and naturally. Relax yourself gradually and start feeling this meditation taking you deeper and deeper.
- In your mind's eye, imagine a beautiful pink bubble forming in front of you. Make the bubble real by seeing it and feeling it with each of your senses.
- Send love from your heart into the pink bubble, filling it with loving and kind thoughts towards the person in distress.
- Remember, the color associated with the heart is pink. Having this color-vibration surrounding what you are visualizing will bring to you only that which is in perfect affinity with your being.

- The next step is to let go of your bubble. Imagine the bubble is now floating up and into the universe to the person that you wish to send it to.
- Imagine this person receiving this "emotional gift" and releasing their toxic emotions.
- That's all you need to do.

Creating a Happy Place, a Simple Self-Hypnosis Exercise

Thoughts really do become things; it just takes a little time for our thoughts to manifest into the physical world. It's important to relax every day, and this simple self-hypnotic exercise can be done by anyone at any time. You can either do it just to relax or you can use the suggestions you created that reflect the life you want to be living. Don't worry if you need to open your eyes during the session to read the suggestions; just close them again and you will go right back into a sense of relaxation.

What exactly is a happy place? A happy place is different for everyone. It should be the most beautiful place you can think of. In fact, it may even be a place that you have never even been. It is important to use your imagination here and all of your senses. See it, feel it, and smell it. If you are on a tropical island, smell the salty sea air. If you are in the desert, feel the warm sun on your skin. If you are on a mountaintop, breathe in the cool, crisp air.

Your mind can take you anywhere you want to go; you just have to see and feel it. This simple technique is a wonderful stress reliever and can be done anywhere or anytime. Don't dismiss this seemingly small exercise. Taking time out of your day to release stress is an important part of any happiness program. Take the time to do this exercise whenever you need. No special equipment is required!

There are many techniques you can use to put yourself into a mild state of hypnosis. It has been said that even light levels of hypnosis can be incredibly effective, so don't think that you need to be in a deep state to elicit change. My intent is not to reinvent the wheel, but to give you some simple techniques to help you create a basic self-hypnosis program.

Self-hypnosis instructions:

- Take a minute to relax and get comfortable. Find a quiet place to sit or lie down, whichever you prefer. This is your time to try to forget about anything that may be bothering you right now. Uncross your arms and your legs.

63

- Take a moment to ensure you are warm, rest your hands loosely in your lap, and take a long, slow, deep breath, feeling the air as it enters your body and becomes warm. Feel the air as it gently travels down into your lungs, holding it in for just a moment.
- As you exhale, feel your body releasing toxins, stress and negativity.
- Focus your eyes on something above your head (perhaps on a spot on the ceiling), so that your eyes become strained, and try to keep them that way, as long as you can, slowly counting backwards from 100.
- When you finally close your eyes, you're immediately taken into a light level of hypnosis. Don't worry if you get tired and don't want to finish counting backwards; that is the idea.
- As you count backwards, continue breathing deeply, holding in the breath for just a moment, before slowly exhaling and emptying your lungs completely, releasing all remaining tension and stiffness.
- Take another deep breath as you count backwards, then let it go, allowing yourself to drift into a state of deep relaxation.

- When you get to the point where you cannot keep your eyes open, close them gently as you let your attention drift.
- Now, imagine yourself at the top of the most beautiful staircase you can think of, and slowly descend at least five stairs. Be sure to count these.
- Feel your feet becoming softer and lighter, as you begin to float into a dreamlike state.
- When you cannot count any longer, or lose the intention to continue going down the stairs, take yourself to your ideal environment for relaxation, or what I call your happy place.
- See your happy place in vivid detail and take a moment to enjoy your environment. See yourself relaxing and enjoying life. Use your power of imagination here, for thoughts become reality!
- You can also give yourself some positive suggestions or use the suggestions that reflect the life you want to be living. Or, simply relax, drift, and dream.
- Tell yourself that these suggestions are now firmly embedded into your subconscious mind where they will grow stronger and stronger each and every day.

- Now take a moment to envision yourself six months down the road, free of this issue or condition. Notice how different you are in this new state of mind. This portion of the visualization is very powerful; take a few moments to see your situation or condition resolved.
- When you are finished, you can take yourself back up the stairway, as you count from one to five.

Steps to Action: Chapter Six

- Take time to enjoy the journey. Don't be in a rush to get to your destination.
- Make a conscious decision to be happy each and every day.
- Practice the pink bubble technique as a meditation or to send someone happy, loving thoughts.
- Take a trip in your mind to your happy place using the simple self-hypnosis instructions.
- Most of all, practice being happy, each and every day, because happiness is a decision.

Conclusion

Congratulations! You're far closer to happiness today than when you first started reading this book. By now, you've discovered the many definitions of happiness, the science behind it, as well as the process of turning bad situations into good. Not only that, but you've gained techniques to live a much happier life. Remember, the way to become a happier person is to read the techniques and to actually use them.

It might be a bit overwhelming if you try to implement all the techniques at one time. For that reason, try them out individually. Make a daily checklist to review at the end of each day and ask yourself if you focused on the areas that you wish to improve on. This will help keep these in focus every single day of your life. Once you improve on a few areas, go back and read this book again. Look at the other ways in which you can improve your overall happiness. The more you practice and apply these methods, the better you'll become. A small amount of change each day starts adding to a significant amount of change over time.

Also, don't just stop with this book. Read additional materials associated with happiness or self-improvement each and every day. The more you read, the better you'll become as a person. These books or other materials of your choosing will always keep you focused on the areas that you wish to improve. If this is the first book you have read on happiness, then congratulations! Your journey has just begun, and you should enjoy it every step of the way.

If you feel this book was beneficial to you, please take the time to add a review on Amazon; by doing so, you will give others the opportunity to find their own path to happiness.

Enjoy the happiness that awaits you!

Visit

EmpowermentNation.com

to view other fantastic books,
and to sign up for book alerts,
giveaways, and updates!

Made in the USA
Columbia, SC
15 June 2017